THE

M

A pocket guide for team members

First Edition

GOAL/QPC and Oriel Incorporated

The Team Memory Jogger™

Development Team

GOAL/QPC

Michael Brassard,
Developer

Bob Page, Project Leader

Dorie Overhoff, Marketing
& Customer Research

Michele Kierstead, Layout
Advisor

Richard Morrison, Chief
Operating Officer

Joiner Associates Inc.

Sue Reynard, Writer and
Project Leader

Barbara Streibel, Subject
Matter Expert

Pat Zander, Marketing

Laurie Joiner, Executive
Vice President

Brian Sullivan, Desktop
Publishing

Jan Angell, Desktop
Publishing

Printed in the United States of America

First Edition
10 9 8 7 6 5

Dear Team Member,

Since the early 1980s, Oriel Incorporated and GOAL/QPC have both been leaders in helping organizations continuously improve their business performance.

We both have publications that organizations have found helpful in creating a more productive workplace through techniques such as process improvement, problem solving, and effective teamwork. The Memory Jogger™ has helped over 5 million customers around the world make fuller use of graphical and statistical methods. The Team Handbook, with more than 700,000 copies in circulation, has helped thousands of teams achieve significant progress.

We have now joined together to create a convenient, practical guide for team members—The Team Memory Jogger™. Here you'll find additional inspiration, information, and tips you need for even more productive teamwork. Please let us know what you think.

Sincerely,

Patricia Ziegler

Michael Brassard   Brian L. Joiner

Acknowledgments

We thank the following people for their contributions to this book.

Mike Adams, *Opryland USA*

Carol Anderson, *Park Nicollet Medical Center*

Davis Balestracci, *Park Nicollet Medical Center*

Daniel Brown, *Busch Entertainment Corp.*

Elaine Engelke, *Public Service Commission*

Bob Faneuff, *Air Force Quality Institute*

Bill Farrell, *Army & Air Force Exchange*

Paul Grunzke, *Air Force Quality Institute*

Kathleen Holm, *Land O'Lakes*

Brian Joiner, *Joiner Associates Inc.*

Kevin Kelleher, *Oriel Incoporated*

Donna Koenig, *Land O'Lakes*

Robyn Kuttler, *Inova Health Systems*

John Lowe, *Sea World of Ohio*

Kimberly Maginnis, *Urgent Medical Care*

Ralph Miller, *S&B Engineering*

Keith Nowack, *Atlantic Steel Corporation*

Antonio Rodriguez, *Department of the Navy*

Dan Sage, *Public Service Commission*

Don Walker, *Toshiba USA*

Table of Contents

Chapter 2: Getting a Good Start

Chapter 3: Getting Work Done in Teams

Chapter 4: Knowing When and How to End

Chapter 5: Problems Within the Team

INTRODUCTION

Being part of a team

By becoming part of a team, you have a chance to help your organization tap into a tremendous reservoir of talent, knowledge, and creativity... YOU! You also have a chance to take advantage of a great learning opportunity.

- You can learn more about your job and the people you work with, as well as your organization and its customers.

- You also have a chance to learn and practice useful work skills.

But working on a team also has challenges.

- For one thing, teams are often brought together to deal with complex or long-standing business problems. So the work itself may not be easy. Periods of rapid progress will likely alternate with periods of frustrating setbacks.

- In addition, coordinating the efforts, schedules, and interests of many people is not simple.

- While some people work on teams full time, most have to juggle team work with their ongoing job responsibilities.

- Though it is exciting to be with people who have different ideas and perspectives, it can also lead to conflict and frustration.

The Team Memory Jogger™ can help you take advantage of the rewards offered by team membership and work through the challenges.

How this book can help

This book contains guidelines that can increase your chances of having a good team experience. It is intended to serve as a quick reminder of things you have already learned through training or experience on the job. The topics are:

- **Preparing to be an effective team member** (Chapter 1, pp. 5-28)
  A team can only be as effective as its individual members. This chapter covers basic skills that can help you contribute to your team.

- **Getting a good start** (Chapter 2, pp. 29-60)
  Many teams get well into an effort without fully understanding why they exist or

consciously deciding how they want to work. This chapter pulls together key issues that teams should work on right up front.

- **Doing work as a team** (Chapter 3, pp. 61-110)
  Many of the basic work skills you already have are useful for working on a team as well. This chapter provides reminders on how to use those skills when working with other people.

- **Knowing when and how to end** (Chapter 4, pp. 111-134)
  It is easy for team members to get so wrapped up in a particular effort that they ignore the signals that indicate it is time to stop and move on to something else. This chapter reviews steps the team can take to end successfully.

- **Problems within the team** (Chapter 5, pp. 135-160)
  All teams run into problems now and then. There are times when people get along and work flows smoothly, and times when people argue and progress stops. Learning how to work through the problem times is critical for having an effective team. While some team problems are quite serious and require help

from outside experts, there are steps that team members can take to help their teams. This chapter provides troubleshooting tips on how to work through team problems

Who is this book for?

This book is targeted at team members—the people who carry out the work of the team. Each topic is examined from the viewpoint of what a team member can do, not what the team leader or a manager should do. The basic information here is relevant to all kinds of teams—project teams, process improvement teams, self-directed or intact work teams, task forces, and so on.

How to use this book

- If you have a specific topic you're interested in, check the Index or Table of Contents.

- To get an overview of what's in each chapter, go to the chapter title pages (they all have a blue edge). Turn the page and you'll see a checklist to help you determine which topic might be useful to you.

CHAPTER 1

PREPARING TO BE AN
EFFECTIVE TEAM MEMBER

Quick Finder

Personal Skills Checklist

Working as part of a team is different than doing a job by yourself. It requires specific skills, many of which you may already have. Take a minute to ask yourself how ready you are to be part of a team.

For example, how often do you...	Rarely	Sometimes	Often
Take responsibility for the success of the team (p. 8)	○	○	○
Follow through on commitments (p.10)	○	○	○
Contribute to discussions (p. 12)	○	○	○
Actively listen to others (p. 15)	○	○	○
Get your **message across** clearly (p. 19)	○	○	○
Give **useful feedback** (p. 21)	○	○	○
Accept feedback easily (p. 26)	○	○	○

You and Your Team

Much of this book talks about things that you and your teammates have to work on together—like creating plans, making changes, solving problems.

But the real foundation of a strong team is strong members: People committed to making the team a success. People who know how to get their ideas across. People who can listen to others and who are open to new ideas. People who are willing to expose and deal with problems rather than hide them under the rug.

Nobody reaches this stage overnight. And no one ever does all these things all the time. But with practice, we can all become more effective team members.

Tips on using this chapter

- Review the checklist on the previous page and evaluate how well you practice these skills.

- Read about the areas you'd like to improve.

- Later on, skim through this chapter periodically to remind yourself of key points.

Taking Responsibility

Why it's important

One of the key things to share on a team is the responsibility for making it a success. Having all team members be responsible is important because…

- Teams often get involved in work that is important to the organization's business success.

- Doing this work well requires the commitment and dedication of all team members.

- Each team member has a unique perspective to offer.
    - Often the best ideas are left unsaid. Your ideas may be critical to helping the team find a workable solution.

What you can do

- **Commit yourself to being part of the team's success**

    – Focus on the team's purpose.

    – Help the team get its work done.

    – Speak out when you think the team is going in a wrong direction.

    – Remember that you are working *with* other people, not against them.

- **Help your team build a common understanding of the issues it faces**

    – Speak up when you have ideas to share.

    – Listen to others and let them influence you; build on ideas already offered.

    – Express your support of others' ideas.

- **Be responsible for what you say and do**

    – Keep your commitments to the team. (See p. 10)

    – Be aware of how your words and actions affect your team. (See pp. 12 and 21)

© 1995 GOAL/QPC, Oriel Incorporated

Following Through on Commitments

Why it's important

Other team members depend on you to get your work done so they can get their work done. Completing assignments on time helps your team make progress and maintain momentum.

> ➤ **TIP** *Ask your teammates, team leader, or manager for help if you have trouble following through on commitments. See if your workload can be temporarily adjusted or if others could help you complete specific tasks.*

What you can do

- **Make your best effort to keep your commitments**

  - Find some way to remind yourself of deadlines and commitments. For example, make notes in a calendar or carry a small pocket-sized notebook.

  - If you cannot follow through on a particular task, let people know as soon as possible so other arrangements can be made.

- **Consider your current commitments and priorities before agreeing to take on more work**

  - Discuss your priorities with your supervisor, manager, or team leader.

  - Though it can be hard to do, saying "no" is more helpful to the team than promising to do something you cannot do.

Contributing to Discussions

Why it's important

The power of teams lies in having people share their ideas and experiences. Much of that sharing happens through discussions. The better your discussion skills, the more you will be able to help your team. These discussion skills are useful in many situations. You'll find them referred to throughout this book.

What you can do

- **Contribute your ideas and suggestions to discussions**

- **Listen closely to others**
    - This is a very important skill. (See pp. 15 to 18)

- **Help *manage* your team's discussions**
    - Help keep the discussions on track.
    - Help involve everyone.

Discussion skills checklist

The list below and on the next page gives examples of useful discussion skills. How many of them do you practice regularly?

○ **I give reasons for my opinions**

"I disagree. I get more complaints from customers about packaging than about delivery time."

○ **I ask others to explain reasons behind their opinions**

"Olivia, could you tell me more about why you think we need a new supplier?"

○ **I help involve other people by asking for their opinions or ideas**

"I'd like to hear what Mary and Tom have to say about what goes on in the production line."

○ **I try to bring the group back on track when discussions wander**

"I agree that figuring out the accounting codes is important, but can we list it as a topic for our next meeting and get back to today's agenda item?"

○ **I pull together and summarize ideas**

"It sounds like all the problems are related to faulty magnetic strips on the new ATM cards. Is that right?"

○ **I suggest methods the group can use to work on issues**

"I'm having a hard time keeping track of all the ideas being raised. Why don't we all take a minute to silently write down our ideas and then go around the table and hear what everyone has to say?"

○ **I help the group check for agreement**

"Do we all agree that we should focus our attention on incorrect entries?"

○ **I try to find areas of agreement in conflicting points of view**

"Michael and Barb, am I right in thinking that you both agree the current computer programs can't do what we need them to do, but that you each have different ideas about what new program we should switch to?"

Listening to Understand

Why it's important

The success of a team often depends on how often and how easily team members reach a common understanding of issues. Listening to understand what your teammates are trying to say is at the very heart of teamwork.

Listening is also an important sign of respect. It encourages your teammates to participate in the team and shows that you value their opinions and ideas.

What you can do

- **Give others your full attention**
  - Resist distractions. Keep focused on the speaker even when other things are going on in the room.

- **Be open to others' ideas**
  - Concentrate on *understanding* the speaker.
  - Accept that the speaker's views, opinions, and values may be different than yours— and might be better!

- **Demonstrate that you are listening**
  - Ask questions.
  - Check your understanding.

    "If I hear you right, Julio, you're saying you object to the changes because you think our time estimates are unrealistic. Is that right?"

- **Combine the ideas you heard with other ideas raised by the team**

  - *Listening* is more than just *hearing* the words someone says. Think about what the person is saying and see if you can relate it to your own ideas or those of your other teammates.

➤ **TIP**   *Take notes. Try to capture the key words as someone else speaks. Don't worry about trying to get every word down.*

➤ **TIP**   *Pay attention to a person's body language. It can help you interpret their words.*

Examples of listening skills

The next two pages provide checklists to help you judge how well you listen. Use them to help you identify areas you may need to improve.

✓ *Listening skills checklist*

You may think you are listening to your teammates, but are you really? Use the following lists to identify areas you may need to work on.

Signs you ARE listening effectively	Rarely	Sometimes	Often
I restate what I think I heard other people say as a way to check for understanding	○	○	○
I give my undivided attention to the speaker	○	○	○
I listen with an open mind	○	○	○
I ask people to slow down if they are speaking too fast	○	○	○
I ask people to explain words or terms that I don't understand	○	○	○

Listening skills checklist, cont.

The checklist on this page can serve as a quick reminder of signs that you are not listening to your teammates.

Signs you are NOT listening	Rarely	Sometimes	Often
I think about what to say next instead of listening	O	O	O
I bring up ideas already suggested	O	O	O
I ask questions that have already been answered	O	O	O
I lose track of a discussion or decisions the team made	O	O	O
I'm sure I know what people are going to say before they say it	O	O	O
I interrupt other speakers	O	O	O

Getting Your Message Across Clearly

Why it's important

As a team member, you have a responsibility to share your knowledge and experience with the rest of the team. To make sure the full team understands your point of view, it's important for you to get your message across clearly.

What you can do

- **Be clear about what messages or points you want to make**
  - Before you speak, try to be clear in your own mind how your points relate to the topic under discussion.

- **Speak in ways that help people understand what you want to say**
  - See the following page for some hints.

- **Be prepared to support your ideas with examples, information, data, or pictures**

Building your communication skills

Speaking in a team meeting can be tough. Fortunately, it gets easier with practice! Here are some tips to help you get started:

- **Speak loudly** enough so others can hear.

- **Keep focused** on key points. Don't ramble.

- **Explain special or unusual terms** you use; avoid jargon when you can.

- **Avoid sarcasm** or "put downs."

- Show how your message **ties into the topic** being discussed.

- Practice making **eye contact** with the people in the room.

   – *This may be hard, but eye contact helps listeners feel more connected to you. It also helps you know if people are lost.*

- **Try drawing a simple sketch** of what you have in mind. Many people understand pictures better than words.

➤ **TIP** Jot down key ideas between team meetings and discuss them with someone else. This helps you clarify your own ideas.

Giving Useful Feedback

Why it's important

Giving feedback means sharing your reactions with a person regarding what they've said or done. Giving feedback…

- Shows that you care about your relationship with the other person.

- Gives you and the other person a chance to work out differences so your team can work more effectively.

What you can do

- **Notice when someone else is doing something particularly helpful to the team**

- **Notice when someone else's behavior or language is making you uncomfortable or disrupting the team**

- **Give these people *useful* feedback**

  - "Useful" means the other person will understand and be able to act on the information you give them. (See pp. 22 to 25)

© 1995 GOAL/QPC, Oriel Incorporated

Building your feedback skills

- *Review the actions and decisions* that led up to the moment.

- Give feedback **sooner rather than later**.

- *Choose an appropriate time and place*.

  – *Be selective about when you share negative reactions in particular. Do it one-on-one and when you will be around to follow up with the person. Hit-and-run feedback is not fair.*

- Start by **describing the context**.
  "I'd like to talk to you about what happened in the meeting today."

- Describe your **reactions and reasons**.
  "I was distracted by your side conversation and couldn't follow what others were saying."

- **Ask for the change** you'd like to see.
  "You often have good points to make and I'd like it if you would share them with the whole group rather than talking over other people."

- **Allow time** for the other person to respond.

Examples of useful feedback

The following pages cover some basic tips on giving feedback. The examples focus on typical feedback statements and how they can be made more useful.

Dealing with the hard stuff

Nobody enjoys telling someone you want them to change their behavior. It's hard to deal face-to-face with someone you strongly disagree with or whose behavior upsets you.

- *Review the guidelines here before you meet with the other person.*

- *Plan out or rehearse what you want to say; jot down notes.*

- *Treat the other person with the respect you would like to be shown.*

- *Ask the other person to meet you where you won't be overheard or interrupted.*

- *Remember that you can only control what you say and what you do. You cannot control the other person.*

Examples of useful feedback

Describe the specific behavior or incident—don't use labels or make judgments

Say this	instead of this
"When you don't do your assignments…"	"When you're irresponsible…"
"It bothers me that you don't let the team have more say in decisions."	"When you act like a little dictator…"
"When you don't speak up, I'm not sure what you're thinking."	"It's obvious you don't care about the team because you don't speak up in our meetings."

Don't exaggerate

Say this	instead of this
"I'm impressed with your work on the customer hotline the past two days."	"Your work is always better than anyone else's."

Examples of useful feedback, cont.

Speak for yourself, not for anyone else

Say this	instead of this
"I am uncomfortable when you and Vic argue at the meetings."	"Everybody hates it when you and Vic argue."
"I liked the way you organized the management report."	"The team liked the management report."
"I was distracted in the meeting by your jokes."	"Pat told me you were telling a lot of jokes in the meeting."

Talk first about yourself, not about the other person

Say this	instead of this
"I'm having trouble knowing how to keep the team on track when…"	"You keep getting us off track."

Accepting Feedback

Why it's important

Just as giving feedback helps other people know
how *they* are affecting *you*, accepting feedback
helps you know how you are affecting others.

What you can do

- **Accept the feedback people give you**

- **Consider this feedback carefully**

    – What are you doing well that you should
      continue doing?

    – What are you doing that might be
      interfering with your team's effectiveness?

➤ **TIP** *Accepting feedback does NOT mean
you automatically agree with the other person
or that you will change your behavior. It only
means you will make an effort to understand
the other person's concerns.*

Building your skill at accepting feedback

Accepting feedback is just as important as giving feedback. Here are some tips.

- **Breathe deeply**. This can help you relax.

- **Listen carefully.**

- **Make sure you understand what the other person is saying.**

  - *You need to understand what the other person wants you to change.*

  - *Ask for examples.*
    "Can you describe what I do or say that seems aggressive to you?"

- **Acknowledge valid points even if you don't agree with the other person's interpretation.** *For example, you can acknowledge that you have been late without agreeing that you are irresponsible.*

- **Acknowledge the feedback but take time to sort out what you heard.**

  - *A simple "Thank you" is all that is needed right away.*

  - *Ask for time to think about what you heard. If possible, schedule a time to get back together with the person.*

CHAPTER 1: ACTION TIPS

Here are some ideas about taking action on the personal skills described in Chapter 1.

- *Don't think you have to become an expert in all these skills overnight. Work on them gradually. Focus on one or two at a time.*

- *Practice the feedback skills at home or elsewhere in your personal life.*

- *Find out what training your company already offers that you are eligible to attend.*

  - *Check with your team leader, supervisor, manager, or training department.*

- *If there is someone in your company who is good at the skill you want to learn, ask them for advice. How did they develop their skills? Can they recommend ways to learn more?*

- *Check if your company has books or videos on the subjects that interest you.*

CHAPTER 2

GETTING A GOOD START

Quick Finder

Start-Up Checklist

Use the following checklist to identify areas your team may need to work on as it gets started. Even if you are not the team leader, you can speak up if you think your team has skipped any of these important steps.

	Yes	No
We have agreed on a **purpose** and written a purpose statement (p. 32)	◯	◯
We have identified the people inside and outside the company who can influence or who will be affected by our work (the **stakeholders**) (p. 37)	◯	◯
We have identified the **limits** and **expectations** for the team's work (p. 44)	◯	◯
We have agreed on the **team roles** (who will have which responsibilities) (p. 48)	◯	◯
We have agreed on **ground rules** (p. 53)	◯	◯
We have decided on **logistics** for when and where we will meet (p. 58)	◯	◯

Getting a Good Start

Keys to Getting a Good Start

What happens before a team gets started and in the first few meetings often determines whether it will be a success. You can help your team get off to a good start by taking an active role in getting everyone to discuss how they want the team to operate.

Tips on using this chapter

- Review the checklist on the previous page as a quick reminder of issues your team should address.

- If you checked any items "No," review those parts of this chapter. Make sure you understand the issues. Review the tips given for what you personally can do.

- In a team meeting or one-on-one with your team leader, ask that these issues be discussed by the whole team.

Agreeing on a Team Purpose

Why it's important to your team

Reaching a common understanding of the team's purpose gives a team a firm foundation.

- It helps everyone understand *what* the team is supposed to do and *why*.

  - If people on the team have different goals in mind, the team can be pulled in many directions at once. This can interfere with the team's work, and some people may become dissatisfied.

- It helps your team define success.

- It can help you establish boundaries for what is and is not included in the team's work. (See p. 44)

  - Knowing what your team is supposed to do helps you understand what it is *not* supposed to do. For example, your team may have been created to implement a solution, not to come up with alternative solutions.

Getting a Good Start
© 1995 GOAL/QPC, Oriel Incorporated

Why it's important to you

Having a clear team purpose also helps you...

- Know what impact the team's work may have on your job.

- Understand the importance of what the team is trying to do.

- Communicate more easily with your co-workers about what the team is doing.

- Focus your thinking and creativity.

➤ **TIP** *Make your team's purpose **visible**. For example, put a sentence about it on your agendas or post it at each team meeting.*

What you can do

- **Find out what your team's purpose is**

  - Ask to see any memos, documents, and data that describe what issues or areas your team should be working on.

  - Support efforts to create a purpose statement.

- **Make sure you understand what that purpose means**

  - Ask your team to discuss the purpose at a team meeting.

- **Use the team's purpose to guide your actions**

  - If you think the team is straying from its purpose, speak up.

Examples of developing purpose statements

The next two pages show the basic ingredients of good purpose statements and some brief examples.

What makes a good purpose statement?

A good purpose statement...

- ***Describes a specific focus** for your team*

  - *It should distinguish your team's work from that of other teams.*

  - *It should let your team understand what work falls within its scope.*

- ***Describes realistic goals***

  - *Goals and targets can help the team make decisions about the level of effort needed. It makes a difference whether the desired improvement is 10% or 50%.*

  - *Goals and targets often come from management. However, your team can still use data on customer needs and business needs to judge how much improvement is needed.*

- ***Is clear, understandable, and brief***

  - *A short statement that everyone can remember is best.*

- ***Is energizing and inspirational***

Examples of purpose statements

The following examples of purpose statements are short enough to be written at the top of agendas or posted in a meeting room. Additional detail should be included in the team's records.

- Provide accurate accounting of employee hours for all Northwest Region facilities

- Fill vacant positions with qualified people within one month of job posting

- Reduce the level of iron contaminate from the current level of 29 ppm to no more than 5 ppm within one year

- Agree on and document the steps for handling accounts with payments more than 30 days past due

- Double the number of new customers from 20 per month to 40 per month while maintaining all current customers

Identifying Stakeholders

Why it's important to your team

Your team's work will affect and be affected by people and groups inside and outside your organization—your **stakeholders.** Knowing who these people are and involving them as you go helps you…

- Understand what is important about your work.

- Identify better solutions to problems and create more buy-in of solutions your team proposes.

- Plan how to include them when your team will be making decisions that affect them.

- Avoid pitfalls and identify limits.

- Know where to get information that will influence your team's work.

© 1995 GOAL/QPC, Oriel Incorporated

Why it's important to you

Understanding stakeholder needs can help you
understand how you can best contribute to your
team. Some stakeholders, for instance, will be
people you work with every day. The better you
can communicate with them about issues that
concern them, the more you can help your team's
work go smoothly.

What you can do

- **Help your team identify its stakeholders
  and understand their needs and concerns**

  - Think about the scope of your team's
    effort and who might be affected by its
    work.

  - Think about groups or people who can
    affect your work, both inside and outside
    the organization.

  - Involve these people as appropriate.

- **Use your knowledge of their needs to guide
  your actions, priorities, and decisions**

> ➤ **TIP** *Don't overreact to what any single group
> of stakeholders tells you. Some of their needs
> may conflict with your team's purpose or with
> your boundaries or limits. Check any conflicts
> with management.*

Examples of stakeholders

The following pages describe four common
stakeholder groups. Use these examples to spark
your own thinking about your team's
stakeholders.

➤ **TIP** *Think broadly about who your
stakeholders are. People in other
departments, for example, might be able to
benefit from your team's work. Groups outside
your organization—such as regulatory
agencies—may influence what options your
team can pursue.*

Managers

What they often care about	Tips for dealing with these stakeholders
• Business results • Customer satisfaction • Schedules • Budgets • Use of resources • Forecasting	• In general, the team leader is responsible for communicating with management about the team's needs and progress. • However, every team member can take advantage of opportunities that come along to keep in touch with their direct supervisor or manager.

Customers

What they often care about	Tips for dealing with these stakeholders
• Quality • Value • Delivery time or turnaround time • Cost • What needs are met by features of your products or services	• Customers are often your most important stakeholders. • See if your organization has existing information about these customers and their needs. • If possible, invite some customers to a team meeting. Better still, visit a customer site to find out in detail how they use your product or service. What do they especially like or not like?

Coworkers

What they often care about	Tips for dealing with these stakeholders
• How they will be involved in or affected by the team's work • What information or support they will be expected to give the team • If they will have to change the way they work	• Communicate regularly with people not on the team. • Explain the what and why of your team's work to them. • Listen to their needs and concerns. • If your team duties mean they have to do extra work, ask your manager if there is some way to ease the burden.

➤ **TIP** *Some organizations encourage people to think of coworkers as "customers." However, the needs of the customers who purchase your products or services are most important.*

Suppliers

What they often care about	Tips for dealing with these stakeholders
• What they are expected to provide to you • If you are getting your needs met • If you will still want to do business with them • If they will be expected to make changes	• Be clear about what you expect of suppliers. • Most suppliers will be eager to work with you if changes are needed. • If possible, invite a key supplier or two to a team meeting or arrange a visit to their site.

Identifying Limits and Expectations

Why it's important to your team

No team gets a blank check to do as much work as it wants anywhere in the organization. Knowing what limits there are and what expectations others have can help your team…

- Meet your organization's business goals.

- Address all the important aspects of the work.

- Minimize conflict or confusion.

- Balance the expectations of different stakeholders.

Why it's important to you

- Some aspect of the limits on the team will affect you personally.

  - For instance, there will probably be limits on how much time you can devote to the team's work.

What you can do

- **Find out what the limits and expectations are for your team**
  - Ask your team leader to discuss these issues at a team meeting.

- **Understand these limits and expectations**

- **Use your knowledge of limits and expectations to guide your actions and decisions**
  - Before taking action or making important decisions, do a quick check to make sure your team isn't exceeding its limits.
  - Periodically ask your team leader or manager if the expectations, purpose, or limits have changed.

Examples of limits and expectations

The following pages show some typical categories of limits and specific examples within these categories.

Examples of limits and expectations

The list below and on the next page gives examples of limits placed on a team.

- **Money/budget**
  There is a budget of $500 for completing the first phase of the work.

- **Time/deadlines**
  This project must be completed by May 30th.

- **Workloads and priorities**
  Team members are expected to put in no more than five hours a week on the team's work.

- **People on the team**
  The project team will have one design engineer, one production supervisor, and two maintenance personnel on it. Other people can be called in as needed.

- **Other people who can be used as resources**
  Curtis H. will be the technical advisor for the team.

- **Training**
  The team can get training only if it can be done in-house and takes no more than six hours.

Examples of limits and expectations, cont.

- **Decision-making authority**
  The team can implement decisions that require less than a $100 investment, provided all potentially affected areas are contacted ahead of time to make sure there are no negative side effects.

- **Access to information**
  The team has open access to all data currently on file. Requests for additional customer data should be forwarded to the sales and marketing departments.

- **Process boundaries**
  Study the order entry process from the time a customer calls until there is a printed bill of lading.

- **Products or areas that will and won't be included**
  The credit vouchers team will look at all vouchers that arise from product returns. It will not study credit vouchers that result from sales incentives.

Defining Team Roles

Why it's important to your team

For any team to function well, its members need to know what is expected of them.

- When people know what their roles are, individuals know what jobs they should do and what jobs will be done by others.

- This helps avoid problems such as no one doing key tasks or one person trying to do everything.

Why it's important to you

Knowing how the work of your team is divided among team members helps you…

- Decide who to communicate with when you have questions or input.

- Understand and keep your commitments.

What you can do

- **Find out how your team is dividing up its work**

- **Understand what is expected of you personally**

  - For example, should you be volunteering to take notes in meetings or to collect data between meetings? Will you be expected to facilitate a meeting?

- **Use your knowledge of roles and responsibilities to meet your obligations to the team**

  - Volunteer for tasks when appropriate.

Formal and Informal Roles

The next three pages describe three formal team roles: team leader, team member, and facilitator/coach. However, many tasks on a team are done informally. People just volunteer to do a particular kind of work such as collecting data, planning a particular effort, or keeping notes. Usually it works best for your team to be flexible in how it divides up its work.

Examples of team roles

Team leader

A team leader guides and manages the day-to-day activity of the team. This involves...

- Educating team members about the team's purpose, limits, etc.

- Tracking the team's goals and achievements

- Anticipating and responding to changes in timing, schedules, workloads, and problems

- Helping team members develop their skills

- Communicating with management about the team's progress and needs

  - This includes re-negotiating limits and discussing priorities, workloads, and resources.

- Communicating with the rest of the organization about the team's actions and achievements

- Removing barriers to team progress

- Helping to resolve conflict

- Taking care of logistics (arranging for meeting rooms, getting supplies, etc.)

Examples of team roles, cont.

Team member

As discussed in Chapter 1 (p. 8), each team member shares the responsibility for the success of the team. As a responsible team member, you should...

- Focus on the purpose of the team

- Think less about personal goals and more about the success of the team as a whole

- Work to develop an atmosphere of trust and respect on the team
    - Treat your teammates with respect.
    - Value different ideas.

- Listen more than you talk

- Communicate clearly

- Participate fully

- Make realistic commitments and then keep them

➤ **TIP** *A team leader is also a team member and should share in the team member responsibilities.*

Examples of team roles, cont.

Team facilitator or coach

Some organizations assign experts in group dynamics, problem solving, or running meetings to help teams. This role goes by many names, such as "facilitator," "coach," and "advisor." Generally, these people focus more on how the team gets its work done than on the content or subject of the team's work.

The work these facilitators do can include...

- Providing training as needed

- Helping the team deal with conflict

- Coaching the team leader or team members on team skills

- Helping the group use basic problem-solving principles and tools

- Leading team meetings, especially when difficult or controversial subjects are being discussed. (See also p. 79)

Agreeing on Ground Rules

Why it's important to your team

Ground rules are guidelines for how the team will function. Having ground rules can...

- Improve the team's effectiveness and efficiency.

- Minimize confusion, disruptions, and conflicts that take away from the real work.

Why it's important to you

- A clear understanding of your team's ground rules can help you know what is expected of you and avoid conflict with others.

- By helping your team set up its ground rules, you can make sure your concerns about how the team operates are taken into consideration.

➤ **TIP** *Each team should discuss and agree to its own guidelines.*

© 1995 GOAL/QPC, Oriel Incorporated

What you can do

- **Find out what your team's ground rules are**
  - If your team has not already defined its ground rules, suggest the issue be discussed in a team meeting.

- **Understand what the ground rules mean**

- **Use the ground rules to shape your own behavior**
  - Participate fully in discussions when the ground rules are being set up. Make sure your ideas and concerns are raised.
  - Stick to the ground rules yourself.
  - Remind the team of particular ground rules when appropriate.
    "Remember that this discussion should be kept confidential."

When rules are broken

All teams violate their own ground rules on occasion. If a ground rule is broken repeatedly, however, you (and your team) need to decide whether or not it's a problem. If it is, consider giving feedback to the rule breaker or discussing the issue as a team. If not, change the ground rule.

Examples of ground rules

This page and the next give examples of typical ground rules.

- **Decision making**
  We will make important decisions by consensus.

- **Use of data**
  As much as possible, we will base our decisions on data.

- **Confidentiality**
  Information shared in team meetings can be shared with others in the organization unless a team member asks that it be kept confidential.

- **Assignments**
  All assignments should be done on time. If you can't get them done, notify the team leader as soon as possible.

- **Participation**
  Everyone will get a chance to voice their opinions.

➤ **TIP** *Be flexible and realistic. Think of ground rules as general guidelines, not rigid laws.*

Examples of ground rules, cont.

- **Meeting ground rules**
  Attendance: We will only meet when a majority of members can be there.
  Starting on time: We will start promptly at 8:30 A.M. Everyone is expected to be here and ready to go at that time, with all the materials and information they need.
  Rotation of roles and responsibilities: We will rotate who will take notes.

- **Meeting evaluation**
  The last 5 minutes of each meeting will be spent discussing how we can improve next time.

➤ **TIP** *Post the ground rules in your team's meeting room.*

Getting a Good Start

The 100-Mile Rule

Once a meeting begins, everyone is expected to give it their full attention. However, it's often hard for people to separate themselves from other work going on. To help coworkers know whether to interrupt the meeting, some teams invoke the "100-mile rule": No one should interrupt the meeting unless it's so important that the disruption would occur even if the meeting was 100 miles away. Be sure you communicate this clearly to your coworkers.

Arranging Logistics

Why it's important to your team

The time available to do a team's work is always limited. Arranging the logistics—such as making sure people know when and where to meet and having the right equipment and supplies available—helps you operate more efficiently.

Why it's important to you

Have you ever wandered around your building wondering just where your team is meeting, or wasted time waiting for someone to track down the right supplies? If so, you know how helpful it is to have the team logistics clearly spelled out.

What you can do

- **Find out where and when your team is meeting**

    - Ask that meeting times and places be discussed at the first team meeting.

    - Make sure you leave enough time to get to the meeting space or work area on time and fully prepared.

- **Help identify and get adequate supplies**

Examples of logistics

The following list includes several of the most common logistical questions that teams need to address.

- How often will the team meet?

- Where will the team meet?
    - Will the meeting place change?

- What time will meetings start?

- How long will meetings last?
    - Will they always be the same length or will it change from week to week?

- How will the team accommodate people who work at different sites or on different schedules?

- Where can the team get equipment and supplies for the meeting?

CHAPTER 2: ACTION TIPS

Here are some ideas about taking action on the start-up topics described in Chapter 2.

- *As a team member, you cannot act alone on any of these issues. The key is to look for ways you can help your team make these preliminary decisions about how it will operate.*

- *Make sure you know the purpose of any team you're on. Ask your team leader if there is a written purpose statement.*

- *Keep track of the stakeholders—customers, managers, coworkers, suppliers—that you are likely to run into on the job. Keep them informed of your team's progress. Try to identify and address potential sources of resistance to the team's activities.*

- *Check to see if each team that you're on has created ground rules for its meetings. If they have, make sure you follow them. If you find any of the ground rules unreasonable, ask that they be discussed at a team meeting.*

CHAPTER 3

GETTING WORK DONE IN TEAMS

Quick Finder

Team Work Methods Checklist

Here is a checklist of basic methods for getting
work done in teams.

How often does your team...	Rarely	Sometimes	Often
Create **work plans** (p. 64)	O	O	O
Have productive **meetings** (p. 71)	O	O	O
Use **data** (p. 87)	O	O	O
Make good **decisions** (p. 92)	O	O	O
Evaluate potential **solutions** (p. 96)	O	O	O
Implement **changes** (p. 100)	O	O	O
Check progress (p. 103)	O	O	O
Document its work (p. 108)	O	O	O

Working as part of a team is different from working on your own. It requires techniques that help teams maintain focus and develop a common understanding of issues. For example...

- Planning helps team members know what is expected of them individually and collectively.

- Effective meetings allow team members to share and exchange ideas and contribute to the team's progress.

- Evaluating alternative solutions helps the team draw on all team members' knowledge and experience, and make better choices.

Tips on using this chapter

The topics in this chapter are arranged roughly in a sequence that matches a team's progress. Planning and having meetings, for instance, come before making decisions and implementing changes. Use the checklist on the facing page to help you find topics that match where your team is.

© 1995 GOAL/QPC, Oriel Incorporated

Creating Work Plans

Why it's important to your team

It's possible to get work done without a plan. We all take actions every day that are not planned. But there are many advantages of planning. A plan...

- Helps a team coordinate the efforts of all the team members—it provides clear direction for team members on what they should be doing and when.

- Identifies targets and deadlines the team should commit to meeting.

- Makes sure key steps in a task or activity are not missed.

- Provides the basis for checking progress.

- Helps you identify potential conflicts in schedules.

- Helps you identify needed resources.

➤ **TIP** *A plan documents what your team wants to have happen. Periodically compare this to what actually happens. Modify your plans accordingly and think about how to create a more realistic plan the next time around.*

What you can do

- **Help your team develop a useful plan**

  - Suggest steps needed to accomplish a given task.

  - Use your knowledge of how work gets done in your organization to help the team estimate how much time and what resources will be needed.

  - Help identify potential barriers that might stand in the way.

- **Use your team's plan to guide your actions**

  - Be clear about your role in making the plan work.

  - Use the plan to identify what work you should be doing and when.

  - Be responsible for completing the tasks that you have volunteered for or that were assigned to you.

➤ **TIP** *If you find yourself doing work that is not part of the plan, check it with your team. Make sure it will contribute to the team's progress.*

Building your planning skills

Knowing how to create a plan is a valuable skill that will help you in all aspects of your work, not just on the team. If you have not done much planning before, here is a list of key steps involved in creating a plan.

- ***Identify what you want to accomplish.***

- ***Identify the main activities*** *or steps needed.*

- ***Estimate*** *about how much* ***time*** *and what other* ***resources*** *are needed.*

  - *How much time will each step take?*

  - *Which people are involved with each step?*

  - *What equipment, supplies, or money will you need?*

- ***Identify measures of progress****: How will you know if the plan is working? How will you know if you are getting the results you need? (See p. 103)*

- ***Create a document*** *that shows the basic elements of the plan. (See the examples on pp. 69 and 70)*

Examples of planning tools

There are many tools that help you capture the basic elements of a plan (listed on p. 68). Two common tools are **planning grids** (p. 69) and **deployment flowcharts** (p. 70).

- A planning grid is often the simplest tool to use. You only need to list the steps or actions down the side of a page and add other important information—such as who is involved and how much time is needed—in other columns.

- A deployment flowchart is particularly useful when the work involves many handoffs between different groups or people.

Basic elements of a plan

The numbers correspond to the plan shown on the next page.

❶Steps or tasks
List the actions, in sequence.

❷Desired outcome
Indicate what each step will accomplish.

❸Who is responsible
Enter the name of the person or group in charge of each step.

❹Planned start and end dates
When should each step start? When should it end?

❺Actual dates
Leave room on the plan to document when the steps actually start and end.

❻Comments
Leave room for capturing notes about what really happens and lessons learned.

❼Other columns can be added
– Budget and expense notes
– Other key people to involve in key steps
– Notes on limits or boundaries
– Hazards or pitfalls

Getting Work Done in Teams

Example of a planning grid

This planning grid shows the first steps a team used to identify and make service improvements.

Step #	❶ & ❷ Step and Desired Outcome	❸ Who	❹ Dates Plan	❺ Dates Actual	❼ time/$$ limits	❻ Comments
1	Search files to identify existing customer data	Otis Marc	Start: 3/15 End: 3/22	3/15 3/27	1 wk/ no $	Computer breakdown on 3/17
2	Contact key customers to understand current needs	Shelly Trisha	Start: 3/23 End: 4/6	3/28 4/7	2 wks/ $500	Good support from marketing made up some lost time
3	Hold meeting to select service improvement targets	Whole team	Start: 4/10 End: 4/10	4/10 4/10		Meeting went well; good prep

Example of a deployment flowchart

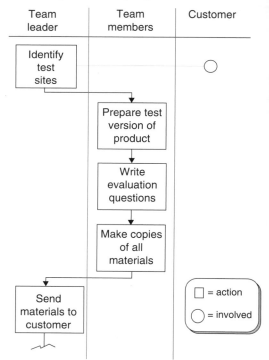

This deployment flowchart captures the basic steps of a plan for conducting a test. It shows the sequence of steps and who is responsible.

Getting Work Done in Teams
© 1995 GOAL/QPC, Oriel Incorporated

Having Productive Meetings

Why it's important to your team

Meetings are often treated as things that "just happen." Poor meetings sap a team's energy and can lead to a slow and painful death. Meetings where the team accomplishes its goals will keep momentum going and contribute to rapid progress.

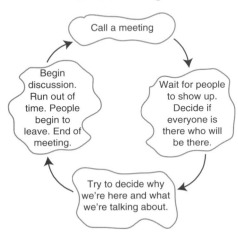

Wrong Way to Hold Meetings

Call a meeting

Wait for people to show up. Decide if everyone is there who will be there.

Try to decide why we're here and what we're talking about.

Begin discussion. Run out of time. People begin to leave. End of meeting.

What you can do

- **Help your team have productive meetings**

  – Use the meeting process (shown on pp. 74 and 75) to help your team create a plan for each meeting.

  – Contribute to discussions.

  – Offer to take notes, keep track of time, or lead a meeting.

  – Contribute ideas for improving your meetings.

- **Work on your own meeting skills**

  – Review the agenda before the meeting and come prepared.

  – Improve your own discussion and listening skills. (See Chp. 1, pp. 12 and 15)

✓ Checklist of meeting methods

The following pages cover some of the most useful tools and methods used to run effective meetings. Which of them do you and your team use?

	Yes	No
We follow a **meeting process** (p. 74)	○	○
We use **agendas** to keep the meeting organized (p. 76)	○	○
We assign **meeting roles**		
Meeting leader (p. 79)	○	○
Notetaker (p. 81)	○	○
Timekeeper (p. 83)	○	○
We **evaluate** our meetings (p. 85)	○	○

➤ **TIP** *The communication skills described in Chapter 1 are also helpful in having good meetings. See the sections on listening (p. 15), discussion skills (p. 12), and feedback (pp. 21 to 25).*

Example meeting process

This two-page flowchart shows a general sequence of events in a meeting. Use it to help you plan your own participation in your team meetings.

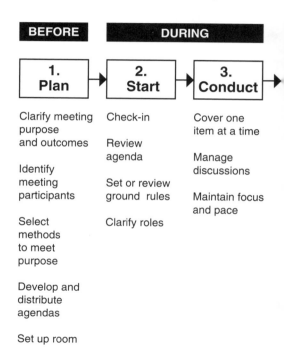

BEFORE

DURING

1. Plan

Clarify meeting purpose and outcomes

Identify meeting participants

Select methods to meet purpose

Develop and distribute agendas

Set up room

2. Start

Check-in

Review agenda

Set or review ground rules

Clarify roles

3. Conduct

Cover one item at a time

Manage discussions

Maintain focus and pace

Example meeting process, cont.

DURING	AFTER
4. Close	**5. Follow Up**

Summarize
decisions

Review action
items

Solicit agenda
items for next
meeting

Review time
and place for
next meeting

Evaluate the
meeting

Thank
participants

Distribute or
post meeting
notes promptly

File agendas,
notes, and
other
documents

Do
assignments

✔ *Meeting agenda checklist*

Meeting agendas help people know what to expect in a meeting. If you are involved in creating agendas for your team, here is a checklist of typical information to include.

○ Items to be discussed

○ Person or people leading the discussion for each item

○ Desired outcome for each item, such as

  – List of ideas or options

  – Shared understanding

  – Priorities

  – Decision or recommendation

  – Action steps

○ Estimated time for each item

○ Meeting evaluation

➤ **TIP**   *You may not need to include all this information if you have regular meetings with standard agenda items (see p. 77). But be sure to include more detail when you are discussing complex or "hot button" issues (see p. 78).*

Example: A simple meeting agenda

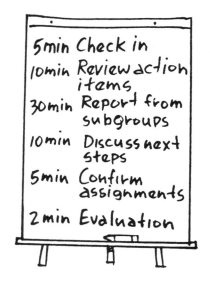

5min Check in

10min Review action items

30min Report from subgroups

10min Discuss next steps

5min Confirm assignments

2min Evaluation

This simple agenda was written on a flipchart at the beginning of a regular team meeting. It has only the items for the meeting with allotted times. It was not sent out ahead of time, and everyone who attends this meeting knows what is meant by these topics so no further detail was needed.

© 1995 GOAL/QPC, Oriel Incorporated

Example: A detailed agenda

Date: Feb 8, 1995		Purpose: Identify job		
Time: 12:30–1:30		reassignments		
Place: Muldowney Room				

TIME	ITEM	WHO	HOW	OUTCOME
12:30	1. Check-in	All	Round-robin	
12:35	2. Review purpose & agenda	Jan	Review	Agree on agenda items
12:40	3. Recap of where we were last meeting	Bob	Report	Establish where we were
12:50	4. Review proposed changes (Attachment A)	Kip	Report & discussion	Understand proposal
1:05	5. Identify concerns and issues	All	Brainstorm	List of what concerns people most

Here is an agenda used at a meeting to discuss job reassignments. The agenda was prepared and sent out ahead of time to all participants. That helped people know what information to bring to the meeting and to come prepared to discuss the issues and share their concerns.

Example: The meeting leader role

Having someone lead a meeting can help keep it on track and running smoothly. The meeting leader...

- Opens the meeting
- Reviews the agenda with the group; makes changes as appropriate
- Makes sure there is someone to take notes and someone to keep track of time
- Moves through the agenda one item at a time
- Facilitates discussions
- Helps the team choose appropriate discussion and decision methods
- Has the group evaluate the meeting
- Gathers ideas for the next meeting
- Closes the meeting

Leading vs. Facilitating

This description of a meeting leader includes "facilitation"—the work that goes into making meetings run smoothly. In practice, other team members often help facilitate the meetings. Teams that are inexperienced or that are having difficult times may benefit from having an outside facilitator or coach brought in to facilitate meetings. (See also p. 52)

Building your meeting leader skills

If you get the opportunity to lead a meeting, here are a few tips to help you out:

- *Take your time.* Your teammates will understand if you need a little extra time to organize your thoughts.

- *Use the agenda as your guide!* A well-organized agenda is a meeting leader's best friend.

- *Ask someone to write key points and action items* on a chalkboard or flipchart in full view of the whole team.

- *Don't be shy about asking for help* from the other meeting participants.

"I'm not sure how to get us back on track here. Can anyone offer some suggestions?"

"Can someone summarize the main points of the discussion so we can capture them in the notes?"

➤ **TIP** *Knowing how to lead meetings is a valuable skill that will benefit all team members. Ask that your team rotate this responsibility.*

Example: The notetaker role

Few people like to take notes at a meeting. Often the problem is that they think the task is more difficult than it needs to be. A notetaker's responsibilities include...

- Capturing the key points for each agenda item.
    - It's seldom necessary to capture everything that is said word for word.

- Highlighting decisions, action items, and issues that will be deferred until future meetings.

- Copying minutes and seeing that they are distributed or posted.

- Filing one copy of the meeting notes in the team's official records.
    - Include copies of any handouts, charts, etc. that were used at the meeting.

Building your notetaking skills

The tips below can help make the job of taking notes much simpler.

- **Speak up** *if you don't understand what is being said or what decision is being made.* "I'm not sure what to put in the notes about this. Is Charlotte agreeing to contact Jerry about getting new equipment?"

- **Use a standard form** *that provides space for the key items your team wants to capture.*

Date: Tuesday, May 31st		
Notetaker: Chris		
Agenda item	**Key points**	**Outcomes**
Data collection	Next week is bad for some but others have free time. The first step is to develop form. Try to get form draft by the 17th.	ACTION: Bobby Jo and Yuri agree to develop data collection form by Friday. Will bring to next meeting for comments.

- **Check if handwritten notes are OK.** *You can often just photocopy the notes for distribution.*

- *If you are more comfortable working at a computer keyboard than writing notes,* **see if your company has a portable computer available.**

Example: The timekeeper role

A team's time together is precious. Yet often when the end of a meeting rolls around the team finds it has not gotten to half of the agenda items. To use meeting time wisely...

- Include times for each agenda item.

- Designate a person to act as a timekeeper.

- Periodically check how close the estimates were to how much time was actually spent on each item.

➤ **TIP**   *Allow flexibility in the schedule. Let the group decide when it's OK to let an agenda item run longer than originally planned and when to cut a discussion short. Do NOT simply police the agenda ("Time's up. Move on.").*

➤ **TIP**   *Help your team be realistic about how much to include in an agenda so you don't always get crunched for time.*

© 1995 GOAL/QPC, Oriel Incorporated

 Building your timekeeping skills

If the responsibility of keeping time falls to you, here are some guidelines you can use.

- **Check** how much time is allotted for an item.

- **Alert** the group when time on any given item is running out.

  "There are two minutes left. Can we wrap up or should we allow more time?"

- **Signal** when time is up.

Example: Evaluating and improving meetings

Taking time to evaluate meetings is the hallmark of a team that wants to make rapid progress. There are several ways to do an evaluation:

- Round-robin comments—go around the room and let everyone share their ideas in turn

- Written evaluations shared with the group

- Open discussion (anyone speaks in any order)

Evaluation questions

- *General questions* about the meeting

  - *What can we do better next time?*

  - *What parts of the meeting worked well?*

- *Specific questions* about issues your team wants to improve

  - *Did we stay on time? Did anyone feel rushed? Did the meeting seem to drag?*

  - *Did everyone contribute?*

  - *Were people open-minded?*

© 1995 GOAL/QPC, Oriel Incorporated

Example: Written evaluation form

Our meeting today was:

| Focused | 1 | 2 | 3 | 4 | Rambling |
| Productive | 1 | 2 | 3 | 4 | A waste |

The pace was:

Too fast   Just right   Too slow

Everyone got a chance to participate:

Yes   Somewhat   No

Our purpose was:

Clear   1   2   3   4   Confused

We made good progress on our plan:

Yes   Somewhat   No

At our next meeting we should:

Do more of:

Do less of:

Using Data

Why it's important to your team

Using data effectively can help your team...

- Identify issues to work on and develop focus.

- Make better decisions.

- Understand the nature and extent of problems.

- Resolve conflicts and differences of opinion.
  "Let's get some data on what our customers say is important."

What you can do

- **Support the use of data on your team**

  - Be open to checking your beliefs and opinions with data.

  - Ask other people if they have data to support their beliefs and opinions.

  - Help identify places where data would be helpful.

- **Improve your own skills in collecting, analyzing, and interpreting data**

Example: Uses of data

The following pages show four uses of data:

- To develop focus (p. 89)
- To pinpoint problems with a process or product (p. 90)
- To investigate possible causes of problems (p. 91)
- To see the effect of changes (included under "Checking progress," p. 106)

 Building your data skills

Being able to collect and use data is another skill that you will find useful in all aspects of your work.

- *Take advantage of any training your company offers on using data tools.*

- *The more experience you can get, the better. Volunteer to help your team collect data.*

- *If you have not collected data before, ask for help from more experienced people.*

- *Practice collecting data on something in your personal life. For example, collect data on your car's gas mileage or your household expenses.*

Getting Work Done in Teams

Example: Using data to develop focus

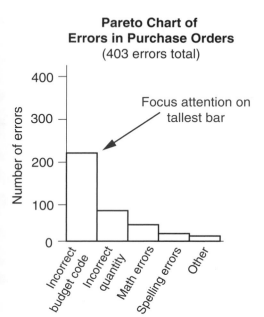

**Pareto Chart of
Errors in Purchase Orders**
(403 errors total)

Focus attention on
tallest bar

The **Pareto chart** above helped a team identify where to focus its improvement efforts. The biggest contributor to problems was errors in budgeting codes.

Example: Using data to pinpoint problems with a product or process

Time plot of moisture content

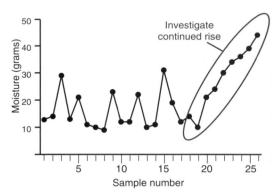

A team that was interested in the amount of moisture in a certain product charted data on a **time plot** (shown above). The appearance of a pattern like the one circled indicates the team should look for something special happening in the process. A time plot is also called a **run chart**.

Getting Work Done in Teams
© 1995 GOAL/QPC, Oriel Incorporated

Example: Using data to investigate possible causes

Scatter plot of test scores vs. number of classes missed

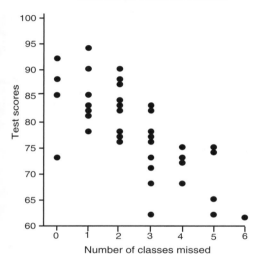

The **scatter plot** above was created by a teacher who wanted to see if attendance in classes really did affect test scores. Though there is some scatter to the points, students who attended more often generally did better than those who did not.

© 1995 GOAL/QPC, Oriel Incorporated

Making Good Decisions

Why it's important to your team

Good decisions don't just happen. Pay attention to how different decisions get made.

What you can do

- **Help to clarify what decision is being made**
  - Ask questions.
    "Is this decision about all overtime policies or just for this one occasion?"

- **Help outline pros and cons of the choices**

- **Help choose a decision method**
  - Different decisions require different levels of support and commitment. (See pp. 94 and 95)

- **Check for agreement**
  - Don't assume that people agree just because they don't speak up. Watch their body language.
  - Formally check with the group periodically.
    "This seems to be our agreement. Is there anyone who is unsure about the choice or other things we haven't considered yet?"

A good decision...

- *Is supported by the people affected by it.*

- *Is based on facts and data, not just opinion.*

- *Is checked against experience.*

- *Is made knowing what the consequences will be (and these have been dealt with ahead of time as much as possible).*

- *Is made quickly enough to meet deadlines but not so quickly that important information and people are ignored.*

➤ **TIP** *To make better decisions, work on your listening and data collection skills.*

Examples of decision methods

This page and the next describe the two most common ways to make decisions: consensus and voting.

Consensus

Consensus means finding an option that *all* team members will support.

- Consensus does NOT mean that everyone is totally happy with the decision.

- To reach consensus you need to consider the ideas, feelings, and situations of *all* team members, not just of a few or even just of the majority.

- Reaching consensus usually takes a lot of discussion time and requires skills in resolving differences of opinion.

- The investment in time is usually worth it, however. Consensus decisions can often be implemented smoothly since they are supported by the entire team.

- Use consensus for complex or important decisions that require the coordination and understanding of all team members.

Examples of decision methods, cont.

Voting

Each team member gets one vote. The choice
with the most votes wins.

> – Voting is easy and familiar.
>
> – It is OK to take a vote for relatively
>   unimportant decisions, but remember it
>   can leave the "losers" feeling left out.
>
> – While taking a vote is a faster way to
>   make the decision, pushing for consensus
>   often makes *implementation* much faster!

➤ **TIP** *Explore important issues by polling. Go
around once and have each member just state
how they vote. Then do a round where people
briefly give one or two reasons for their vote.*

Delegating decisions

*In some cases, the team may let one or a few
team members make a particular decision.
This works well when the decision requires
particular expertise or when time is short.*

*"Chris and Zola will be responsible for getting
input from the whole team, but then they can
make the final call on which vendors to use."*

© 1995 GOAL/QPC, Oriel Incorporated

Evaluating Potential Solutions

Why it's important to your team

Many teams rush to implement the first solution that comes to mind. However, it's usually better in the long run to evaluate a number of possible solutions before making any changes. This helps a team choose the best option and be creative in combining the best aspects of several options.

What you can do

- **Help your team identify and evaluate potential solutions**

    - Generate a list of criteria *before* you discuss the options so you'll know how to interpret your discussions.
    "Do we go with Option A because it's cheaper? Or is it better to go with Option D because it's quicker?"

    - Brainstorm possible solutions. Be creative.

    - Evaluate solutions against the criteria.

Getting Work Done in Teams

- **Be as objective as possible**
  - Gather information on the strengths and weaknesses of all proposed solutions, including your favorite.
  - Be open to new perspectives.
  - Think creatively about how to address concerns others have with your favorite solution.
  - Be willing to combine parts of different solutions.

Examples of ways to evaluate potential solutions

The following pages show examples of several techniques for evaluating the pros and cons of different solutions.

- The **solution checklist** (p. 98) provides an overview of information you may find helpful

- The **solution matrix** (p. 99) is a quick way to capture key points for each potential solution

➤ **TIP** *Allow people time to think carefully about pros and cons of different alternatives and to check ideas with others not on the team. Often this means continuing the discussion over several meetings.*

✅ *Solution checklist*

Here is a checklist of common criteria used to evaluate proposed changes or solutions.

○ **Cost**

  – Dollars, time, additional investments needed (new equipment, for example)

○ **Impact** on the organization

  – Which employees will be affected and how

  – Training needed

○ **Potential benefits**

  – Improvements customers will see

  – Savings in time, money, or hassles

  – How the change will help position the company better for the future

○ **Potential problems**

  – Anticipated problems and potential prevention or remedies

○ **Ease of implementation**

➤ **TIP** *This information can be summarized in a **solution matrix**, like the one shown on p. 99.*

➤ **TIP** *Use data as often as possible.*

Example of solution matrix

The solution matrix below shows options a company considered when deciding whether to replace a receptionist who was leaving or find a new way to handle incoming calls.

Solution	Cost	Benefits	How Hard or Easy	Potential Problems
Send all incoming calls directly to customer service area	2 hrs technician time to reprogram & test phones 30 minutes training for C.S. staff $0	Does not require additional staff Uses current technology Get a person answering the phone	Easy Can implement immediately	Callers could wait in queue several minutes while C.S. reps. are taking orders or answering questions
Hire a new receptionist	Salary and benefits $200 advertising	Continue providing fast responses to incoming calls Get a person	Moderately easy Will take 6 weeks to	Filling receptionist position means staffing needs in C.S. won't be met

Implementing Changes

Why it's important to your team

Coming up with ideas about what needs to be changed is often the easiest part of a team's work. Making the changes takes planning, follow-through, and cooperation. Doing it well will increase the odds that your team will see its ideas put to good use. Not doing it well may mean all your hard work will go to waste.

Two keys to making changes well are **planning** and **communication.**

- Good plans help your team manage its resources and time.

- Good communication helps changes go more smoothly and makes sure nothing important is missed.

The power to make changes

Some teams have the power to make changes in the workplace, usually within certain limits or boundaries (see p. 44). Others are asked just to come up with recommendations. Before making changes, be clear about your team's limits and authority.

What you can do

- **Help draft a plan for making the changes**

- **Help implement the changes**

    – Identify what role you can play in making the changes happen. Follow through on your commitments.

    – Volunteer for tasks such as updating training or work documents.

    – Discuss proposed changes informally with coworkers. Explain how and why the changes are being made and how it will affect them. Listen to their concerns.

    – Pay attention to what happens when the changes are made. Look for things that are working well or aren't working well, and for both intended and unintended effects.

- **Give the changes a chance to work**

Example of ways to make changes

The next page describes one method that can be used to make changes.

Example of a method for making changes

- Develop a **plan.** (See p. 64)

  – Be sure to identify ways you will know if the change is working.

- Try the change on a **small scale**.

  – Look for ways to test the change with only a few people or in a small part of the work area.

  – Carry out the change and check to see if it worked.

  – Identify ways to improve the change.

- Implement the changes **full-scale**.

  – Document how the new or updated procedures should work.

  – Train everyone in the new procedures.

- Periodically **check** on how well things are working. (See p. 103)

> ➤ **TIP** *Much of the time, you will get some resistance to the changes your team wants to make. Involving other people in planning and implementing these changes can greatly reduce resistance.*

Checking Results and Progress

Why it's important to your team

Many teams fall into a trap of making changes and assuming they will get the results they wanted. Effective teams, however, know that it's critical to monitor results, check progress, and modify the changes as needed.

What you can do

- *Before* the change, help your team understand the current situation

    – What happens now in the workplace? Volunteer to help collect data or other information.

- Help to identify "measures of progress"

    – What will be different if the change has the desired effect? (See p. 105)

- *After* the changes, help your team collect new data

    – Prepare "before" and "after" charts displaying the results. (See p. 106)

Examples of ways to check progress

The next few pages describe some helpful techniques for checking progress.

- First, identify **measures of progress**. (See p. 105)

- Create **simple displays** of "before" and "after" data. (See p. 106)

- Track results by adding an extra column to your planning grid (discussed earlier in the chapter, p. 68), or create a new **check form**. (See p. 107)

Examples of measures

The key to identifying measures of progress is to think about how you will know if your purpose is being achieved. For instance, what will be…

- different?   – improved?
- increased?   – reduced?
- eliminated?

Here are a few specific examples of what you could measure:

- Number of hours to produce a specific document
- Number of days in the hospital after surgery
- Reasons for phone calls to the customer support line
- Number of defects per thousand pieces a machine produces
- Percent reduction in time to complete a process
- Percent increase in equipment uptime

➤ **TIP** *Review your team's purpose statement. It should give you clues on what to measure.*

Example of using data to check progress

The chart below shows how many foul shots a
basketball player made out of each 30 tries
before and after training. The data values from
after the training are clearly much higher than
before the training.

**Number of baskets made out of
each 30 tries, before and after**

Before		After
	25	
	24	
	23	
	22	● ● ●
	21	● ●
	20	
	19	● ●
	18	● ● ● ● ●
●	17	● ● ●
●	16	●
	15	● ● ●
●	14	
● ● ● ●	13	
● ● ●	12	
● ● ● ●	11	
	10	
● ●	9	
	8	
● ●	7	
	6	
	5	

Example of a form used
to check progress

Step	Completion Dates		Hours	Comments
	Plan	Actual		
#1. Develop training materials	2/3	2/12	28	Discovered we didn't agree on steps
#2. Test with 3 people	2/22	3/1	8	They wanted more diagrams
#3. Improve materials	3/8	3/8	4	

This simple form was used by a team to track the progress of its plan and to document follow-through of key issues.

This basic form can easily be adapted to let a team capture more details on information such as amount of improvement made, cost savings, and so on.

Keeping Records and Documentation

Why it's important to your team

During a team's lifetime—be it weeks, months, or years—members will discuss countless issues, look at a lot of data, take many actions, and so on. Accurate records of what your team does and accomplishes helps maintain forward momentum and prevent rework.

What you can do

- **Help your team keep accurate and complete records**

  - Volunteer to take notes at meetings or organize the results of data collection efforts.

  - Make sure information you help to gather is captured in your team's records.

Examples of team records

The list below shows four of the most common types of team records, but you may have others.

- Notes from meetings

- Data records, including graphs and charts

- Results of customer surveys

- Reports summarizing the team's progress and achievements

CHAPTER 3: ACTION TIPS

- *Remember that you share responsibility for the team's success. Contribute to discussions, help develop plans, offer opinions when the team is making decisions, and so on.*

- *Take every chance that comes to you to develop your personal skills in these areas. The more of these skills you have, the more valuable you will be to your organization.*

- *Encourage your team to experiment with different kinds of decision making. See what works best in different situations.*

- *Develop simple data-based measures to track your own work. For example, take data on how long it actually takes to complete tasks compared to what you thought it would take.*

CHAPTER 4

KNOWING WHEN AND HOW TO END

Quick Finder

Closure Checklist

The following checklist covers the main signals that tell a team its current effort should be brought to a close. How many of them apply to your team?

	Yes	No
We **accomplished our purpose** (p. 114)	O	O
We took steps to **maintain the gains** (p. 116)	O	O
We **completed the documentation** of our actions, results, and ideas for future improvements (p. 120)	O	O
We **evaluated** our work (how we worked together and what we accomplished) (p. 124)	O	O
We **shared results** with others (p. 126)	O	O
We **recognized** everyone's contributions and **celebrated** our achievements (p. 132)	O	O

Sooner or later, every team has to end something. Project teams, for instance, may be finishing their work while ongoing teams may just be completing a particular effort. The question is *how* you want to end. Letting achievements go unrecognized can be disheartening. To end on a positive note...

- **Evaluate and document** the team's work, achievements, and lessons learned.

- **Maintain the gains:** Take steps to make sure the changes and improvements made by the team will continue.

- **Share results** with your organization.

- **Recognize and celebrate** the contributions that made the team's achievements possible.

Tips on using this chapter

The methods described in this chapter cover the main themes mentioned above. Use the checklist on the facing page to help you decide which of the items your team has completed and which need further attention.

Knowing You Have Achieved Your Purpose

Why it's important to your team

If your team does not know how to tell when its purpose is accomplished, it could end up stopping too early or too late.

- If a team's work ends before sufficient progress has been made, your organization may suffer business losses.
  - This often includes increased costs, quality that is less than it could or should be, failure to meet customer needs, rework down the road, and so on.

- If it continues for too long, the organization pays in other ways.
  - For example, the team may have missed out on other improvement opportunities by focusing too long in one area.

Being able to judge when you have accomplished your purpose helps your team and your organization use its resources wisely.

What you can do

- **Help your team identify appropriate indicators or signals**

    - The time to figure out how you will know when you are done is at the *beginning* of a project or effort. (See Chp. 2, p. 44)

    - Think about what will be different when you are done. What will be better? What will be happening or not happening? What will the data look like? (See Chp. 3, p. 104)

- **Help your team recognize when its purpose has been accomplished**

    - Regularly review the data and other information your team is gathering.

    - Compare this information to indicators you have identified.

    - Let your team know when you think it has made sufficient progress.

Maintaining the Gains

Why it's important to your team

Many teams have been disappointed when they realize that improvements they made have been lost. Teams need to do whatever they can to make sure the changes they have made are preserved.

What you can do

- **Help your team identify changes that will make it easy for people to use new procedures and hard for them to backslide to the old methods**

  - Help document exactly what is being changed. Who has to do what and when?

  - Think about how the procedures can be made error-proof. What could prevent people from using old methods? What will make it easy to use the new methods?

- **Help to update appropriate documentation**
  - Identify any job aids used to do the work. This includes manuals, diagrams, flowcharts, computer records, or other work instructions.
  - If you have the authority, update these job aids as needed. If not, come up with recommendations for your manager or supervisor.

- **Help to develop a plan for getting the new methods well established**
  - Include a plan for trying out updated training, procedures, and documents on a small scale.

Example of updated job aids

The following pages show a job aid that helped people use a new procedure.

- A **deployment flowchart** can show people how different tasks relate. This sample also includes space for brief notes on what should be measured on this process and what actions to take as a result.

Example of form for maintaining gains

The form on these pages was used to help

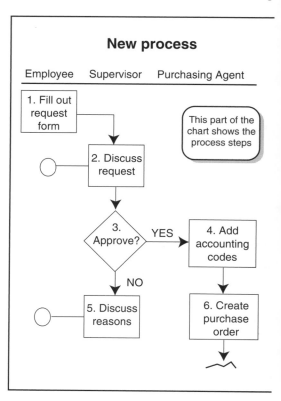

New process

Employee	Supervisor	Purchasing Agent

1. Fill out request form

2. Discuss request

This part of the chart shows the process steps

3. Approve? — YES → 4. Add accounting codes

NO

5. Discuss reasons

6. Create purchase order

Knowing When and How to End

© 1995 GOAL/QPC, Oriel Incorporated

from changes made to a process

people manage a purchasing process.

Measures	Actions
(Who tracks what)	**(What to do about it)**

> This part of the chart shows how to monitor the process and what actions to take

3. Supervisors track # of requests approved and denied.	3. Create chart showing monthly figures. Alert manager if rises abruptly or over time. Look for patterns over time.
4. Purchase agent counts # of requests where it is not clear what code to use.	4. Alert supervisor if not clear what code to use. Develop new codes as needed. Revise request form.

Completing Your Documentation

Why it's important to your team

A team's documentation serves as the *organization's* memory of what happened on the team—what was learned, what was gained. Having every team document its efforts is a key ingredient in creating rapid learning and progress.

What you can do

- **Help your team update and complete its records**

    – Help your team keep track of achievements, successes, and lessons learned.

    – When it's time to end, help to compile and organize all the pertinent records.

    – Review the documents to make sure *you* understand them.

➤ **TIP** *Pretend it's a year down the road and you want to refer to something your team did. Will you understand the language, references, and plots in your team's documentation?*

© 1995 GOAL/QPC, Oriel Incorporated

Example of completed documentation

- The following two pages show excerpts from a **storyboard**. This kind of documentation relies mostly on pictures, graphs, and brief comments to capture the key points of a team's effort.

These two pages show excerpts from the beginning
project. The complete storyboard ha

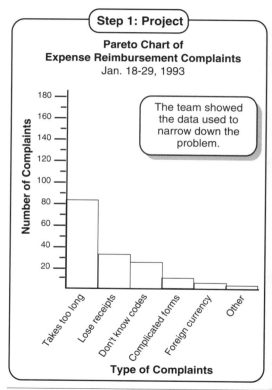

Step 1: Project

**Pareto Chart of
Expense Reimbursement Complaints**
Jan. 18-29, 1993

> The team showed
> the data used to
> narrow down the
> problem.

Number of Complaints (y-axis: 20, 40, 60, 80, 100, 120, 140, 160, 180)

Type of Complaints (x-axis: Takes too long, Lose receipts, Don't know codes, Complicated forms, Foreign currency, Other)

Type of Complaints

and end of a team's storyboard on its reimbursement
information on many other steps.

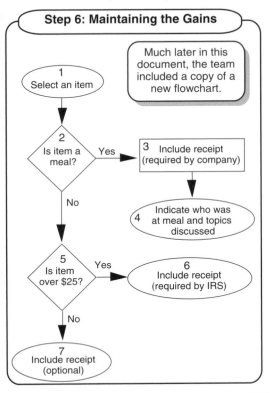

Step 6: Maintaining the Gains

1
Select an item

Much later in this
document, the team
included a copy of a
new flowchart.

2
Is item a
meal?   Yes →   3 Include receipt
(required by company)

No

4 Indicate who was
at meal and topics
discussed

5
Is item
over $25?   Yes →   6
Include receipt
(required by IRS)

No

7
Include receipt
(optional)

Why it's important to your team

Though one effort or project is coming to a close, every person on the team will probably be involved with other efforts or teams in the future. Taking time to evaluate the current effort or project…

- Helps provide a sense of closure.

- Reinforces key learnings.

- Provides the basis for ongoing improvement.

What you can do

- **Help your team evaluate its work**

  - Before the meeting when your team is going to evaluate its work, review your own documents. Jot down notes on things you liked and didn't like about the results the team achieved or how the team did its work.

  - Encourage other people on the team to do the same.

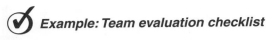 **Example: Team evaluation checklist**

The checklist below shows steps often taken to
evaluate a team's work.

○ **Start with a general evaluation**

- Have everyone share their overall
  impressions.

- What did the team do well?

- What did the team have trouble with?

○ **Review the team's achievements**

- Did you accomplish your stated purpose?

- If yes, what made that possible?

- If no, what roadblocks stood in the way?

○ **Compile a list of key learnings**

- What did you learn about the product,
  service, or process that you worked on?

- What did you learn about your customers
  and their needs?

- What did you learn about working
  together as a team?

○ **List ideas for how future efforts could be
  improved**

Knowing When and How to End   **125**

Sharing Results

Why it's important to your team

You and your teammates have probably learned a lot by being part of the team. It may be obvious that sharing your lessons with others not on the team can benefit *them*, but how can sharing results benefit *you*? Sharing your work...

- Helps reinforce the lessons you have learned.

- Can make the final implementation of your team's ideas go more smoothly.

What you can do

- **Help your team share its results formally with the organization**

    - Identify ways that information is shared in your organization.

    - Help your team use these outlets to publicize your accomplishments.

- **Share lessons and insights informally with your coworkers**

    - Talking with coworkers can help them feel more involved with the team.

Examples of ways to share your results

There are many ways that your team can share its results with the rest of your organization. Two of the most common, described on the following pages, are to...

- Do a presentation. This is most often done for a manager and coworkers, but is sometimes done for executives or customers. (See p. 128)

- Contribute an article to your organization's newsletter. (See p. 130)

➤ **TIP** *See if your organization has a central database, file, or record-keeping system for tracking team efforts. If so, give a copy of your team's documents to the people who maintain those records.*

Example: Preparing a presentation

- Work with your teammates to decide who will be involved in developing and delivering the presentation. **Try to involve everyone**.

- Find out who will be in your **audience.** What do they need to know? How will they use the information you give them?

- **Write notes** about what you want to cover.

  - Include a brief review of what your team did, what it learned, and what impact the work will have or has had on the organization and its customers.

  - At the end, be sure to include recommendations for next steps.

- **Make it visual**. Many people understand charts and pictures better than words.

  - For instance, put key charts, data, or sketches on flipcharts, posters, or overheads.

- **Practice the presentation**

  - This is especially important if the whole team is involved. A practice session lets everyone coordinate their timing and key points they need to make.

Knowing When and How to End

➤ **TIP** *If your team's work has involved contact with customers or suppliers, try to involve them in the presentation as well.*

Knowing When and How to End   129
© 1995 GOAL/QPC, Oriel Incorporated

Example: Writing a newsletter article

Many organizations use in-house newsletters to spread information. The editor of this newsletter would probably be happy to publish the results of your team. Here is a simple outline you could use for the article.

1. Introduction

- Describe the problems or issues the team addressed and what solutions were put in place.

- Give a brief overview of actions and results.

➤ **TIP** *Open the article with a story from a customer or coworker who was experiencing the problem your team solved.*

2. Summary of major findings

- List or briefly describe the steps the team took.

- Describe the changes the team made and what the results of those changes were.

➤ **TIP** *Use data charts and diagrams to show what the team discovered.*

3. Lessons learned

- Describe what the team learned about the specific issue being studied and its impact on the organization's business needs and its customers.

- Include notes on what the team learned about how to plan, analyze problems, make changes, and so on.

➤ **TIP** *Focus on tips you think will help other people in your organization.*

4. Acknowledgments

- List all the people on your team and acknowledge the support of your departments and managers.

- Include anyone who was not on the team but who contributed to its work (by covering phones or doing extra work, for example).

➤ **TIP** *BE GENEROUS. Include anyone who supported your team's efforts.*

➤ **TIP** *Have someone take a photo of your team at work, or of the product or workplace you studied.*

Recognition and Celebration

Why it's important to your team

Everyone likes to have their contributions to an effort acknowledged. This includes not only the team members but others who helped the team. Recognizing and celebrating the team's achievements helps to reinforce the positive feelings that come from working together to solve problems.

What you can do

• **Help your team recognize everyone's contributions and celebrate everyone's efforts**

– Keep track of people inside or outside your organization who have supported the team's efforts. Make sure these people are acknowledged by the team—invite them to the party, send them thank-you notes, post their names on a bulletin board, etc.

Principles of recognition and celebration

- *Recognize and celebrate **learning** and **contributions**, not just "successes."*

  - *Many teams do not achieve success as defined by their original purpose statement. If they document and learn from their efforts, they have gained valuable knowledge for their organizations.*

- *Keep it **simple**.*

  - *Examples: give an informal party with pizza or cake, bring doughnuts for breakfast, post a notice or article on a lunchroom bulletin board, give out token gifts such as t-shirts.*

- *Be **inclusive** rather than exclusive.*

  - *Include people who covered for team members, those who helped collect or analyze data, and so on.*

  - *Include people who will carry on the team's work, such as coworkers who will be implementing the changes.*

  - *Include customers, suppliers, or others outside your organization.*

Knowing When and How to End

CHAPTER 4: ACTION TIPS

- *Try not to get so caught up with your team that you ignore signals that tell you it's time to end—such as achieving your purpose!*

- *Recognizing and celebrating **all** contributions can make it easier for the team to disband.*

- *Recognize and celebrate significant **milestones** along the way. Celebrate early and often!*

- *Try out different ways to celebrate and recognize achievements. See which work best for your team and your organization.*

CHAPTER 5

PROBLEMS WITHIN THE TEAM

Quick Finder

Checklist of Common Problems

Listed below are some common problems that
occur within teams. If any of these sound like
your team, look further in this chapter to see
what you can do to improve the situation.

If this sounds like your team...	See ...
Several people fight over everything	Conflict,
Even small arguments turn into fights	p. 138
The boss is on the team and people will not speak openly	Power, p. 144
Everyone goes along with what the expert says, no questions asked	Experts,
When the expert speaks, no one can figure out what s/he's saying	p. 146
People spend most of the meeting time telling personal stories	
People often talk about several different topics at the same time	Focus, p. 149
We have about 15 things going on and never get anywhere on any of them	
No one on our team ever disagrees	Agreement, p. 154
One team member talks all the time while others hardly say anything	Participation, p. 156
A lot of people don't finish assignments	Follow-through, p. 158

Most teams go through natural and expected cycles of highs and lows: excitement one moment when hard work pays off, frustration and anger the next when progress stops because of disagreements or confusion over the team's direction. The first step is to recognize that *some* conflict and disagreement within a team is a good sign!

- To make good choices and decisions, a team must balance the often conflicting ideas that people bring to the table.

- If there is never any disagreement on a team, it probably means people are not being honest or open about what they really think.

It's not always easy to know when a problem you see on your team is natural and normal—and something that will pass—and when it's a serious problem that needs attention.

Tips on using this chapter

Use the checklist on the facing page to identify symptoms that sound like the problem your team is having. Then review the appropriate pages in the chapter.

Handling Conflict and Disagreement

Symptoms

- **Feuding**

  - A few members fight over every topic discussed.

  - People insult and attack each other personally rather than discuss ideas.

  - People push each other into corners by exaggerating or using highly judgmental words.

- **Disagreements**

  - Emotions run high, making it hard for people to work together to resolve issues.

  - Legitimate differences of opinions tend to become win-lose struggles. People are more concerned about winning the argument than finding a path forward for the team.

Why it's important to deal with conflict and disagreement

Some amount of conflict shows that members are testing ideas and trying to come up with the best path forward. But in some cases, conflict reaches a critical stage, such as...

- When two or more team members are feuding—disagreeing and arguing over everything just for the sake of argument.

- When every disagreement is taken as a sign of unhappiness with the team or an unwillingness to get along.

In these cases, the team should actively work to reduce conflict so the team can make progress.

What you can do

- **Help your team deal with feuds that are interfering with its progress** (See p. 140)

- **Help your team find common ground when disagreements erupt** (See p. 141)

- **Be aware of your own responses to conflict and try to find ways to be less emotional when you disagree with others** (See p. 143)

Tips on dealing with feuds

- Recognize that the feud may have started long before the team existed and may outlast it. Don't try to end the feud; try to find a way to let the team move forward.

- Suggest discussion methods such as round-robins and silent "thinking" time to prevent feuding members from dominating a meeting with their arguments.

- Encourage the adversaries to discuss the issues outside of the team meetings.

- Tell the feuders about the effect they have on the team.
  "When you two go at each other, it wastes the team's time and makes it difficult for anyone else to participate without taking sides."

- Ask your team leader or manager to help members deal with their differences.

Problems Within the Team

Tips on dealing with disagreements

- Listen carefully to each person's point of view.

- Help to clarify the core issue by separating areas of agreement from areas of disagreement. (See p. 142)

- Suggest discussion methods such as round-robins and silent "thinking" time when feelings start to run high.
  "Let's all take five minutes to think silently about these issues and jot down our ideas. Then we can share them with the group."

- Periodically check your understanding of the disagreement. (See also Chp. 1, p. 12)
  "As I understand it, we agree that the payroll system is the first priority, but we disagree about whether a new computer is needed. Is that right?"

Here is a practical way to help identify the real issues during a disagreement.

- Draw a vertical line on a large sheet of paper or chalkboard.

- On one side, write down what people agree about. On the other, write down what they disagree about.

- See if the differences between the sides are important for the team's work. If yes, help develop a plan for getting information that will help resolve the issues. If no, move on.

Problems Within the Team

Tips on ways to be more objective

- Keep your comments **focused on the topic**, not on the person who disagrees with you. Say "Here's why I think that approach won't solve the problem…" instead of "Jillian, you don't understand the issues."

- **Avoid judgmental language.** Say "Here's what I'm concerned about…" instead of "That's a stupid idea."

- Make an honest effort to **understand the other person's point of view**. Ask them for more detail before giving up on their ideas. Say "I don't think I understand how your suggestion would solve the problem, Bea" instead of "I don't think that's relevant."

- If you find yourself constantly fighting with another team member, **ask for help** from your team leader, manager, or a facilitator. Do not let your feud harm the team.

- See also the section on giving feedback, p. 21.

Problems Within the Team   **143**

Dealing With Power and Authority

Symptoms

- Once a manager or expert states an opinion, everyone falls in line.

- Managers or supervisors discourage discussion about their areas of expertise or authority.

- People comment that they don't say what they think "with the boss around."

Why it's important to deal with power and authority

People with more power or authority than other team members can be a valuable resource. However, they can become a barrier to progress when their power or expertise stops criticism of their opinions. This can be a problem because the soundness of all ideas should be tested before they are adopted by the team.

(If the person with more authority *wants* people to challenge his or her opinions, but the team members are afraid to do so, see "Too much agreement," p. 154, for ideas on what to do.)

        Problems Within the Team

What you can do

- **Help your team avoid situations where one person's power or authority squashes contributions from other team members**

  - When setting up the team's ground rules (see Chp. 2, p. 53), suggest a ground rule that "strengths and weaknesses of all ideas will be discussed before decisions are made" or "all job titles will be parked at the door."

  - Try to make sure this ground rule is enforced consistently for *all* team members, not just for the person with the power or authority.

- **Speak up when you think someone's power or authority is hurting the team**

  - Ask your team leader to talk to the person outside of a team meeting. If the problem is with your team leader, speak to him or her first or ask a manager or supervisor for help.

Dealing With Overbearing Experts

Symptoms

- Experts discourage discussion about their areas of expertise.

- Experts use technical jargon or refer to complex principles without explaining things in plain English.

- Team members follow the expert's advice without any challenges or questions. They consider no other perspectives.

- If a team member questions an expert, or offers a different opinion, other team members may brush those ideas aside and try to silence the differences of opinion.

Problems Within the Team

Why it's important to deal with overbearing experts

Many teams deal with complex issues in the course of their work. Having experts on the team can…

- **Help** by providing team members with a deeper understanding of the technical aspects of their work. In this way, experts can contribute significantly to the team's success.

- **Hurt** if they discourage discussion of their recommendations or seem to believe that their advice need not be explained. This can leave team members confused and frustrated, and may mean the team will miss important information that would have emerged from open discussions.

For team members to support the team's work, they must have the chance to discuss all issues.

➤ **TIP** *Remember, too, that a non-expert can often provide a fresh viewpoint that will give a team new insight on a problem or situation.*

© 1995 GOAL/QPC, Oriel Incorporated

What you can do

- **Help your team use its experts wisely**

  – Do not let your team substitute "expertise" for "discussion." The expert's ideas should be input to the team's thinking.

  – Ask for technical terms or concepts to be explained in simpler words.

  – Ask the expert to draw a picture.

  – Ask the expert to present the data to the team and explain what it means.

  – Ask for the expert to have a segment of the meeting time to teach the other team members key information that would help in the team's work.

  – Ask to hear everyone's reactions to what the expert says.
    "Could we go around the room and each say how these ideas match our own experiences?"

© 1995 GOAL/QPC, Oriel Incorporated

Lack of Focus

Symptoms

- **Floundering or wandering off the path**

  - No one knows what is most important to focus on.
  - Members discuss several topics at the same time.
  - People lose track of what the discussion is about.
  - People say the same things about the same topics that they've said in previous meetings.
  - Discussions never get completed before a new topic gets started.

- **Too much to do**

  - Too many things to work on all at once.
  - So much going on that there is little progress on anything.

- **Too many distractions**

  - People spend more time telling personal stories, joking around, taking phone calls, etc., than on the team's task.

© 1995 GOAL/QPC, Oriel Incorporated

Why it's important to have focus

Teams need a sense of progress and momentum to feel successful and enthusiastic about their work. When the team fails to focus on its work, members can become frustrated, bored, or lose interest, and may even stop doing the work or coming to meetings.

Part of the trouble is that it's very easy to *lose* focus—there are a lot of factors that can get a team off track!

What you can do

- **Help your team develop and maintain focus** (See p. 151)

- **Help your team narrow its focus when there is too much to do** (See p. 153)

- **Help your team overcome distractions** (See p. 153)

➤ **TIP** *There will always be many issues competing for the team's attention. Revisit your purpose statement periodically to remind yourself about your team's focus.*

Tips on keeping focused

- Make sure your team is clear about its purpose, deadlines, limits, etc. (See Chp. 2)

- Use agendas to keep track of what should and should not be covered in each meeting. Ask that the purpose statement be printed at the top of every agenda. (See Chp. 3, p. 76)

- When the team has been off track for some time, suggest moving back to the task.
  "Where are we in finishing our work today?"

- Suggest that you discuss one issue at a time rather than several simultaneously.
  "Can we finish choosing our measures before looking at data collection forms?"

- Ask if someone can summarize the discussion up to this point.

- Find a way to keep track of issues you want to temporarily set aside.
  - For example, put ideas not related to the topic under discussion on a separate flipchart (sometimes called a "parking lot"). (See p. 152)

Example of a "parking lot" flipchart

During a discussion of changes to a purchasing process, this team kept track of related issues that came up but that they didn't want to deal with immediately. These issues were added to the agenda for the next meeting.

Parking Lot Issues
- Screening criteria for vendors
- Training on new maintenance procedures
- Work assignment changes

Tips on narrowing focus

- Use data to identify the most important thing to focus on first—look for problems that occur most frequently, have the most impact, or that customers care about most.

- When new issues or opportunities arise, check them against your team's purpose and plans. Will working on that issue contribute to the team's progress?

Tips on overcoming distractions

- Ask that there be an agenda item for personal "check-ins" at the beginning of your meetings (try for no more than 5 minutes). This can help people make the transition from "other work" to "team work."

- If people start telling stories during the meeting, help to bring the focus back to the task at hand.
  "I think we're running out of time for this topic. Could someone recap where we were so we can close the loop?"

Problems Within the Team   **153**

© 1995 GOAL/QPC, Oriel Incorporated

Too Much Agreement

Symptoms

- Nobody disagrees.

- Once a position is outlined, everyone focuses on why it's right. No one raises objections.

- No alternatives are offered and different perspectives are quickly dismissed.

Why it's important to have some disagreement

When team members want to get along above all else, the team can fall into "groupthink." Everybody automatically goes along with a proposal even when they secretly disagree. This can lead to bad decisions because ...

- Critical information is withheld from the team. People decide their concerns are not relevant.

- Ideas are accepted without careful consideration of their pros and cons.

What you can do

- **Help your team avoid groupthink**

  – Suggest the team brainstorm a list of options before discussing any course of action in detail.

  – Speak up if you have a different point of view.

  – Remind members that all ideas should be thoroughly examined and understood by everyone.

  – Develop a list of criteria and help the group systematically apply the criteria to all the options.

  – Suggest that the team ask a "devil's advocate" to raise objections to a solution.

➤ **TIP** *Once an option is selected, brainstorm everything that could go wrong with that choice. Discuss ways to prevent potential problems and to avoid risks that are identified. Then decide if additional information is needed.*

Uneven Participation

Symptoms

- Some members talk too much.

- Others talk too little.

Why it's important to balance participation

To be successful, teams need input from every member.

- When some members take up too much airtime, others have less opportunity to explain their points of view. People who talk too long can keep a team from building momentum and can make some team members feel excluded from the team's work.

- At the opposite extreme are members who say almost nothing. They may be quiet because they have a hard time breaking into the discussion, or because they need some silence to find the words they want to say. It's important for the team to find ways to invite their input.

What you can do

- **Help to establish the ground rule that it's important to hear from everyone in the group**

- **Speak up when *you* have something to say**

- **Suggest methods for hearing from others in the group**

  – Suggest going around the group in turn so everyone can get a chance to offer a viewpoint.

  – Ask quieter members for their viewpoints.

  – Ask if the team could break into subgroups to discuss some issues, then have the subgroups come back together to share their ideas.

  – Ask that everyone take a few minutes of *silent* thinking time so that people who find it hard to speak up can have time to organize their thoughts.

Lack of Follow-Through

Symptoms

- Tasks don't get done on time.

- People don't do assignments between meetings.

- People won't volunteer to do tasks.

Why it's important to have follow-through

Teams cannot make good progress without much of the work occurring between team meetings. This means that members must volunteer for tasks and be responsible for completing them. When this doesn't occur, the team bogs down and loses momentum.

What you can do

- **Volunteer for tasks that need to be done and schedule time on your calendar to do the work**

- **Ask for help from your team leader or other team members if you cannot complete a task**

  - Take advantage of being on a team! Your fellow team members might be able to juggle their workloads and responsibilities to help you get done on time.

- **If you don't have enough time between meetings to do team work, talk to your supervisor or manager**

  - In most cases, team responsibilities are something you have to do in addition to your regular job. If your workload gets overwhelming, it's worth a try to speak with your manager or supervisor to see if your priorities or responsibilities can be changed temporarily.

Problems Within the Team   159

CHAPTER 5: ACTION TIPS

- *Do not let group problems fester! The longer you ignore them the worse they will get—guaranteed!*

- *Keep in mind that the purpose of trying to solve group problems is so your team can get its work done. You are not there trying to make everyone get along like best friends! Keep focused on the team's work.*

- *As much as possible, avoid blaming individuals. Think of problems as **group** issues, not as something that affects only one or two people. Try to think of ways that the whole team can work together to minimize disruptions and conflict, to keep focused on its work, etc.*

- *Learning to deal with group problems is seldom easy, but you can get better at it with some practice. However, don't be afraid to ask for help! Dealing with serious problems may require the intervention of a trained specialist.*

- *The clearer your team is about its purpose, and the more you use data and practice good listening and feedback skills, the better you'll get at preventing problems.*

Index

Notes

Support your team's continuous improvement efforts with

The Memory Jogger™ II

The Memory Jogger™ II is the most cost-effective way to support your teams in problem solving and effective planning. Today, more than 5 million people are using the tools in the **original** *Memory Jogger™* and the **new** *Memory Jogger™ II*. And, 90 of the Fortune 100 companies are using these pocket guides as their resource to support internal quality efforts. Make *The Memory Jogger™ II* an integral part of your quality programs by including your company's logo, mission statement and other information. 164 pages. $6.95. Call for information on quantity discounts and customization options.

Call **GOAL/QPC** at
1-800-643-4316
Phone: **508-685-6370**   Fax: **508-685-6151**

Oriel Introduces
The Team® Trail Guide

A true interactive CD-ROM designed specifically for new team leaders and those with seat-of-the-pants experience. It covers the essential topics for new team leaders to get off to a good start.

- Recognizing what it means to be a team
- How the role of team leader is different from team member
- The 7 keys of successful teams
- The 4 components of effective team communication
- How conflict can be an opportunity
- An 8-step plan for conflict resolution

This CD-ROM is filled with real team leadership scenarios and examples. Give your team leaders an edge. Call Oriel today and order *The Team® Trail Guide*.

1-800-669-8326 or 608-238-8134
www.orielinc.com

an oriel incorporated publication,
core methodologies group

We'd Like to Know What You Think
of *The Team Memory Jogger™*

Your opinions about this product are important to us. Please return your completed survey by mail or fax to the address on the back cover of this book. Thank you.

1. How did you hear about this new book?
- ❏ Oriel Incorporated Product Catalog
- ❏ GOAL/QPC Product Catalog
- ❏ Complimentary *The Team Memory Jogger™* preview guide
- ❏ Coworker
- ❏ Magazine advertisement
- ❏ Other

2. What do you like most about this book?

3. How will you use this book? Check all that apply.
- ❏ Training reference
- ❏ Personal reference
- ❏ Other _____
- ❏ Post-training reference
- ❏ Coaching/mentoring

4. What could we do to make this a better product for you?

- ❏ Please add my name to your mailing list.
- ❏ I prefer not to be added to your mailing list.

Name _____

Title _____

Company _____

Address _____

City_____

State _____ Zip _____ Country _____

Phone _____ Fax_____